If I Were A Racist:

Exploring Racism in Music Teaching

First edition published by Holders Hill Publishing in 2024

Copyright © Nathan Holder, 2024

The right of Nathan Holder to be identified as the Author of the Work has been asserted by him in accordance with the Copyright, Designs and Patents Act 1988.

A Cataloguing-in-Publication catalogue record

for this book is available from the British Library.

Paperback ISBN 978-1-7395839-5-8

CONTENTS

Dedicated to the memory of
Jarritt Ahmed Sheel

Education is an important element in the struggle for human rights. It has the means to help our children and our people rediscover their identity and thereby increase their self-respect. Education is the passport to the future, for tomorrow belongs to those who prepare for it today.

– Malcolm X

Foreword

I remember coming across Nathan Holder's poem 'If I Were a Racist' back in the summer of 2020. Here, in the United States, we were undergoing a tectonic shift in race relations brought about by the murder of George Floyd on May 25, 2020. We saw most Americans, with allies around the world, call for racial and social justice. My family and I attended protest marches in New York City, where I live, and I watched as American structures and institutions struggled to grapple with the systemic racism that had shaped my country for hundreds of years. Now, in 2024, the pendulum has swung the other way in the U.S., and simple efforts to diversify structures and include all peoples are under attack. Who could've imagined that 'diversity,' 'equity,' and 'inclusion' could ever become such dirty words—but here we are. And because of the ongoing battles to define how we interpret our racist past, *If I Were a Racist: Exploring Racism in Music Teaching* is such a welcome addition to the growing antiracist literature in music education.

I generally avoid the tripwire word 'racist' in my writings since so many readers tune out upon seeing that word, and I remember being impressed with Holder's usage. It drew me in and challenged my own beliefs about race at the same time. Now, in his compelling *If I Were a Racist*, Holder expands on and explains what he tried to convey in the initial poem. Taking each stanza of the poem as an epigraph to a chapter, Holder unpacks what he meant in the poem and creates a framework for the given chapter. Further, by centering the experiences and epistemologies of BIPOC people, Holder helps the reader, irrespective of racial identity, analyze their own understandings of music and music education.

For instance, in highlighting music's overemphasis on a few European languages, primarily French, German, and Italian, Holder writes, 'It's a shame that one of the things that might make young people feel as though they can't continue their studies in music, isn't the music itself, but the language required to talk about it' (p.20). By highlighting such exclusionary tactics, which in the past have been used quite consciously by musical white-supremacist structures and institutions, Holder creates a space for dialogue with other music educators and for (self)reflection, which is made even easier by the blank pages that follow each chapter intended specifically for such reflection.

In something of an exhortation, toward the end of the book, Holder states that 'A music education that understands all music has emerged from the world and deserves to be treated equally and studied through its own lens' (p.91). Ultimately, his is a call to action, a call to treat all music of our planet with equal dignity and equal humanity. This short book will challenge you to think deeply about your own beliefs about music and music education and will help you chart a path toward a more inclusive and richer musical experience for yourself and your students.

- **Philip Ewell**

Introduction

The poem that this short book is based on was published on the 26th of June 2020, just over a month after the murder of George Floyd in Minneapolis, USA. In the immediate days following his death, and coinciding with the start of the global pandemic, I decided to write this poem, expressing some of my thoughts, feelings, and research around race, white supremacy, and music education. Many people around the world had been discussing matters about race with a particular intensity, that eventually saw many (mostly white people) feeling fed up with the constant conversations, questions, and accusations.

All of my music teachers in school and university were white, and I owe every single one of them so much. I would not be the musician and educator I am today if it wasn't for them. However, questions remain about the things which, despite my privileged musical education, I missed out on. I missed being able to connect my understandings and experiences playing in church with what we were required to do in class. Like many of my peers at the time, we consumed hip hop (especially from the USA) but never in the classroom. There were even moments when I realised that everyone would look at me and the other Black boy in our music class every time Jamaica or reggae music was discussed. These seemingly small occurrences affected me in different ways, and no doubt form part of the reason why the poem and this book exist. I will always wonder how things may have been different, and I continue to wonder about those who didn't have the extra help and opportunities I had.

When some music educators first encountered this poem, there were many misunderstandings about what it meant. There were educators who took it as a direct attack on themselves and their professionalism — after all, no one likes being called 'a racist', or would think that their profession, in any way, could be inherently and/or institutionally racist. This poem in some ways added fuel to this smouldering fire, and it was discussed and removed from a Facebook group, not before many insinuations and aggressive language were directed towards me.

This is one of the problems in talking about race. It can be very difficult for Black, Brown and Indigenous educators to be honest about their thoughts and feelings when it comes to race, knowing that the very mention of the word racism results in many people instantly taking that defensive stance of 'I'm not'. Many of us have been educated in the same systems and ideas we now critique, which creates its own internal conflict, battling against imagery and sound, which is simultaneously native and foreign. All this while existing, learning, and teaching in White spaces, means constantly having to shift, adjust and hide so as not to appear as though our internal dialogue is not telling us to run in the opposite direction. Nevertheless, we are still here, trying in various ways to highlight, critique, and create through lenses of social justice, anti-racism, and decolonisation.

Rooted in European colonialism and imperialism, the belief that white Europeans were the dominant racial group on earth, resulted in white supremacist thought and action, which manifested in how the world was shaped during and after the European colonial era. These practices helped to form the idea of race: a social construct which has and continues to have global consequences.

This poem was written from the standpoint of what someone might say, do, or think, someone who was invested in maintaining whiteness as the dominant frame of reference, thought, and practice in music education. In essence, if 'I were a racist', these are some of the things I would do to maintain my dominance and power in music education, even if I seem to be progressive and inclusive. In this way, you can substitute the phrase 'If I Were A Racist', for 'If I Were A White Supremacist', to see if that makes a difference in how you think about the content of the poem and the explanations. This poem is far more about how racism creates structures and institutions, than it is about verbal or physical assaults. On occasion while offering explanations, I use the term 'ourstory' instead of 'history'. I hope that by using this term, I encourage you to think about the interconnectedness of stories, rather than the ways in which we are often taught, of history isolated from our present realities.

Unfortunately, many of us unwittingly perpetuate some of these racist ideas every day. Pointing these things out is not (always) done to assign blame, but to help show us how white supremacy surrounds us, and how difficult it can be to embed anti-racist practice. As you read this book, I invite you to reflect on how some of these ideas manifest themselves in your practice, settings, schools, or institutions.

In this book, I am choosing to centre the experiences and epistemologies of Black, Brown and Indigenous peoples and our many intersections. This book is intended to be a broad overview of many issues, and the nuanced experiences of all racially marginalised peoples requires further and more detailed interrogation. The hope is that this book, along with other resources, can be used as a launchpad into the details of how racism and white supremacy manifest in music education.

Chapter 1

If I were a racist

If I were a racist,
I'd teach children that talking about music means,
Texture, timbre, and tempo.
If you can't use these words, you're not a musician.

If I were a racist,
I'd teach reggae music and Bob Marley,
'Stir It Up', but never 'War'.
I might even mention marijuana.

If I were a racist,
I'd insist that all music was taught from notation,
Removing all the nuances
That paper could ever express.

If I were a racist,
I'd teach 'African' drumming.
Because of course,
Africa is a country.

If I were a racist,
I'd teach that the Great Composers were
Mozart, Beethoven, Haydn and Bach,
Not Miles Davis, Florence Price,
Alice Coltrane and J Dilla.

If I were a racist,
I'd make sure that Gospel, Blues and Jazz,
Were always taught,
As music created by slaves.

If I were a racist,
I'd call all non-white music
'World Music'.
After all, it's them and us.

If I were a racist,
I'd ignore that Mozart, Beethoven, Haydn, Bach
And the Trans-Atlantic Slave Trade
Happened at the same time.

If I were a racist,
I'd make sure that violins and pianos
Were seen as more important,
Than steel pans, tablas and didgeridoos.

If I were a racist,
I'd teach 'African' songs,
Without knowing what they mean,
Or where they were really from.

If I were a racist,
I'd standardise everything –
You're either in tune,
Or you're out. Literally.
If I were a racist,
I'd have posters of me on the walls and in the books.
No black or brown faces,
Just my own.

If I were a racist,
I'd make you think including one brown face,
Would be enough.
Diversity. Inclusion.

If I were a racist,
I'd be fine with all white exam boards,
And all white teaching staff,
And study all white musicians.

If I were a racist,
I would insist that children learn Western music notation,

Forgetting that many civilisations,
Flourished without it for centuries.

If I were a racist,
I'd put up black squares,
And messages about standing together.
Then never invest in anti-racism training for my staff.

If I were a racist,
I wouldn't address outdated policies
Or really let black and brown people
feel safe enough to speak on their experiences.
If I were a racist,
I'd know that,
Even though the notes may be black,
The spaces would remain white.

Chapter 2

Language

If I were a racist,
I'd teach children that talking about music means,
Texture, timbre and tempo,
If you can't use these words, you're not a musician.

Using words to describe music isn't easy. After all, how do we describe something that we can't see, touch, taste, or smell? We all perceive sound differently, depending on our musical understandings, physiology, cultures or even our ages. For example, have a listen to the opening of Pink Floyd's *Great Gig In The Sky*, or the beginning of *The Message Continues* by Nubya Garcia. To describe these songs in English, you might use words like slow, groovy, energetic, or sad, rather than words such as thin, andante, or homophonic. In the right contexts, some of the words we use in music education (at last in English) serve a very specific purpose, but outside of the classroom, many of us go back to the words that we use in everyday life.

One of the problems with using 'technical' words such as diminuendo or arco, is that using this unfamiliar language can be a struggle for children who aren't used to hearing, reading, or using these words and phrases at all. I hear what you're thinking

— 'we have to learn words in biology or chemistry, so what's the problem in music?'

When we use Latin words or other technical phrases in biology, for example, we are talking about very specific things. For healthcare to be effective, we need to be specific about the particular arteries, parts of the eye or brain. Doctors cannot afford to be general about parts of our anatomy or always give general diagnoses, hoping that a specific problem will be solved.

It's also important to remember that many words we use are rooted in one language — Italian. Why Italian?

During the 10th century in central Europe, Latin was the main written language, used by the church and state. As staff notation evolved over the next few hundred years, it coincided with Italian becoming an established language, and with many of the most well-known composers of European Renaissance style music being Italians. They wrote their instructions in Italian, and this practice was adopted and spread around Europe, and eventually the world. Italian (and to a lesser extent, French and German) has become the default language to describe specifics in music education. In reality, there is no legitimate reason why Swahili, Spanish, or Korean words couldn't be used to describe music in Kenya, Spain, or Korea, for example.

The issue is not that these words exist, or are taught, it is that sometimes we don't allow the flexibility for students not to use these words. It's a shame that one of the things that might make young people feel as though they can't continue their studies in music, isn't the music itself, but the language required to talk about it. If some of these words and phrases are barriers to not only learning, but progressing in music education through exams, then it's a problem that needs addressing. Why? Because in the wider music industry and in performance, it's much more common to hear words and phrases such as 'different colours', 'lighter', 'sit in the pocket', 'change the vibe', 'more touch', 'bigger', 'hold back a bit', and 'build up'. To do their job as effectively and efficiently as possible, doctors need specific language. To be a musician or music educator, we have the scope to be as flexible as we'd like. Being this flexible presents a challenge in music education because of the ways in which these words and phrases are embedded into many exams and curricula. Change may be seen as music education 'lowering standards'; a loaded phrase which requires the retort of, 'But whose standards are you talking about?'

If one of the purposes of music education is to give students a broad understanding of the world of music, the emphasis on students using language most commonly associated with European classical music (in some cases, for music that didn't even exist during the European classical era) and its analysis needs to be addressed.

Reflections

Chapter 3

Bob Marley and Reggae

If I were a racist,
I'd teach reggae music and Bob Marley,
'Stir It Up' but never 'War'.
I might even mention marijuana.

How can teaching students about reggae music and Bob Marley be considered racist or uphold white supremacy?

During the 1970s, Bob Marley and his band The Wailers, helped to export the reggae music created on the island of Jamaica around the world, inspiring people from every single generation since then. Teaching about Bob Marley isn't inherently racist. However, in many ways Bob Marley has become a token — it is not uncommon for lessons on reggae to start and end with Bob Marley, excluding other reggae stars past and present, including Gregory Isaacs, Koffee, and Tarrus Riley. In doing this, many students are never exposed to the wide range of reggae that has existed. Aside from this, what is taught and what is avoided can expose how whiteness has been embedded into pedagogy, even when the musician or music is from the Global South.

Composed in 1967 by Bob Marley himself, *Stir It Up*, was went on to become one of Bob Marley and the Wailers' most recognised songs. It's a great track to teach certain elements of music such as chord structures, rhythms, and baselines that make up that late 60s rocksteady/early reggae sound, which is why it is so widely taught and explored. It's a love song, full of sweet lyrics and accompanied with tight harmonies from gentle backing vocals. On the other hand, *War*, released in 1976 is one of Marley's most politically charged songs. Although the songwriting credit has been disputed over the years, the lyrics reflected Marley's own worldview, being taken from a speech given by Haile Selassie I in 1963. The significance of talking about Marley but ignoring songs such as *War*, *Zimbabwe*, and *Exodus*, lies in the fear of discussing anything — political or otherwise — that may 'distract' from the music itself. Especially with music from the Global South, many lyrics of a political nature can be critical of the legacies and systems of oppression created by European colonialism, which are foundational to how, when, why, and by whom the style was created in the first place.

But should music education only be concerned with the music and not the lyrics of a song? Surely it is in the basslines, chord progressions, and musical forms that real and essential learning takes place?

The lyrics of songs, such as those mentioned above, teach us so much more than musical elements and provide invaluable context for students to understand what the term 'musician' means to different people. Helping students to see and understand that musicians have had key roles in helping to shape and comment on the geopolitics of the day can give a new sense of meaning for students who are conscious about how they can use music to make a difference in their worlds. The lyrics of *War*, for example, can help deepen understanding of how some peoples from across the Black African diaspora were and are, heavily invested in the political struggles and cultures of Black Africans from across the continent.

Of course, one of the barriers to this way of thinking and approaching music education is how equipped teachers are to talk about potentially triggering or sensitive subjects. Not only that, but what about the political ramifications of attempting to allow anything to enter the classroom which didn't conform to the current mainstream political ideology?

If teacher training does not evolve to embrace elements of critical pedagogy, opportunities to broach subjects that may help students understand themselves and the world around them may be lost. It requires us to examine how whiteness can prevent us from studying music which, in different ways, exposes the effects that racism and colonialism have had on our world.

Reflections

Chapter 4

Learning By Ear

If I were a racist,
Insist that all music was taught from notation,
Removing all the nuances
That paper could ever express.

Learning by ear is the way that the majority of people around the world learn music. From steel pan players in Trinidad and Tobago, tabla players in India and pop musicians, ways to create and learn various styles of music doesn't always involve deciphering lines and dots on a page.

The Western notation system is a good system for the styles of music it evolved to represent, especially European classical music. This way of musicking spread around the world during and after the era of European colonialism and imperialism, and has accelerated in the last 60-70 years, due to technological advances and globalisation. With the dominance of certain Western cultures dictating how many educational institutions design and execute their programs, learning music from this type of notation has become the focus.

This has had large repercussions. The choice to teach from notation meant that it was in large part the people who could read and teach this notation system who became music teachers, lecturers, and researchers. As generations of music students came and went, this cycle continued. Coupled with European classical music being the dominant form of music in the academy, those who flourish in music education are often those who can read and play in that style. Not only that, but those who benefitted from this system and had careers outside of music education (even outside of the music industry) have always been able to advocate for this way of teaching and learning. These days, it is not uncommon for politicians (for example) to extoll the benefits of music education, often referring to the European classical style ensembles and instruments, which would have undoubtedly required them to have attained a certain comprehension of Western music notation.

For a lot of music originating outside of the Global North (and even some styles emerging from within it), this means that music often has to be contorted to fit into this Western system, and in the process, can lose some of its nuance and meanings. Learning and playing by ear is how many pop, church, and blues musicians learn, not to mention the many different folk styles to be found the world over.

While there are many examples within curricula and examinations that require aural training (i.e. interval and cadence recognition), it is the processes of listening, picking out specific parts, blending with other musicians, changing key spontaneously, and applying all these lessons to performances that takes a back seat with the focus on European classical music and learning staff notation. The focus on this way of musicking, therefore, prohibits peoples who do not possess the finances or certain forms of cultural capital from becoming music teachers, and being able to teach ways of learning based on their own experience and expertise.

There is also a capitalist element to this. The global market for sheet music was valued at just over $361 million in 2022[1]. If there were to be a sudden focus on learning by ear, it could result in significant revenue losses by publishing giants such as Breitkopf and Härtel, Warner Music, and Hal Leonard. There would be knock-on effects for examination boards, and it would require investment into many kinds of resources, training for teachers, and an overhaul of many curricula and examinations. Capitalism and colonialism have historically been intertwined, and the white supremacist attitudes, which have excluded epistemologies and ways of musiking in the Global South, can often be traced by analysing who controls the production and distribution of materials used within (in this case) music education.

1   Market Growth Reports (2023) *Global Sheet Music Market Size, Star and Industry Analysis by regions, Countries, Types, and Applications, Forecast to 2028.* Market Growth Reports.

Reflections

Chapter 5

'African' Drumming

If I were a racist,
I'd teach 'African' drumming.
Because of course,
Africa is a country.

'African drumming' is a phrase that has been used for decades in music education. Many students and teachers know what the phrase represents, especially if we have participated in 'African drumming' ensembles, taught them, created or consumed resources on the subject. But what is it about this phrase that makes it problematic?

Africa

Africa is the second largest continent on earth and has a long history of being referred to as though it is a country. It's a reductive stereotype which began — again — during the era of European colonialism, where part the mission for many white imperialists was to civilise the 'savages' in Africa, extract resources, and set up strategic military bases. Through literature, media, and scientific racism, for decades Africa has frequently been depicted as a place only filled with poverty, disease, and famine. Even songs which were created to help Africa such as *Do They*

Know It's Christmas (released in 1984), helped to perpetuate this same stereotype. There are still people today who think that there is a language called 'African'. It is commonplace to see 'African music' workshops taking place in educational settings, as well as 'African music' used in commercial settings.

The reality is that Africa is incredibly diverse and larger than many of us were taught. It is made up of 54 sovereign countries[2], each with many different languages, cultures, histories, and economies, and is comprised of a land area larger than the U.S.A., China, India, France, Germany, and Spain *combined*.

Drumming

Imagine for a moment that you encountered a poster or advert that encourages you to join a string ensemble.

What does 'string ensemble' mean?

The term is not specific enough to refer to a particular style of music, and there are many different types of stringed instruments that require different techniques and tuning. Erhu? Harp? Kora?

We are accustomed to being very specific when we refer to certain styles or ensembles. A string quartet, jazz trio, or gospel choir conjures up specific images or sounds. It also places music in a rough period — there were no gospel choirs in the 13th century, and jazz (or Black American Music) didn't exist how many of us now conceptualise it until the 20th century. String quartets span

---

2   African Union Mission to the United Nations (2020) *The Africa Group at the United Nations*. African Union. https://www.africanunion-un.org/africangroup#:~:text=The%20Africa%20Group%20at%20the,States%20at%20the%20United%20Nations. (Accessed 23 Oct 2023).

a longer period of time, but we can still locate them in time — circa 18th century. Even saying this, the phrase 'string quartet' could refer to any ensemble featuring four stringed instruments, but it has been almost exclusively used to refer to an ensemble comprised of two violins, a viola, and a cello (with variations).

What about a European string ensemble?

The question becomes where in Europe, and also, which stringed instruments?

So, for 'African drumming' — where in Africa, and which type of drums?

In practice, African drumming usually sees many children playing djembe drums, playing syncopated rhythmic patterns, which often interlock, and utilising call and response techniques. Many children around the world have benefitted from these lessons, learned about rhythm and how to play with others. However, these ways of learning and teaching can perpetuate the idea that Africa is a country and that djembe drums are the instrument of choice on the whole continent. Because of how Africa, its music, and instruments are talked about and grouped together, there is more chance of students of any age being able to name 10 orchestral instruments, than 3 from the African continent.

When we use terms such as 'African drumming', we are effectively saying that there is one style of drumming from Africa. There are hundreds, if not thousands of different kinds of drums in Africa, and numerous styles originating in West Africa alone.

Renaming 'African drumming' to 'West African drumming' is a step in *a* direction, but it still only goes so far. It is a reminder that drums and drumming approaches in Egypt, Mauritania, Zimbabwe or Ethiopia are very different, as one would expect given the size and diversity within the continent.

In the same ways that we are specific about Baroque or Romantic styles of music and the instruments of the European style orchestra, we should aim to be more specific about the rhythms and styles that come from the continent of Africa and that span hundreds, if not thousands, of years.

Reflections

Chapter 6

The Great Composers

If I were a racist,
I'd teach that the Great Composers were
Mozart, Beethoven, Haydn, and Bach,
Not Miles Davis, Florence Price, Alice Coltrane, and J Dilla.

The skill required to craft a piece of music from nothing, or piece something together from existing materials is incredible. Amazing music in different forms has been made by 8-year-olds and 98-year-olds alike, and it can take years for someone to establish a particular sound or aesthetic to separate them from the millions of musicians past and present. It's usually those people who have managed to change the way we think, experience, or enjoy a certain style or ensemble who we end up referring to as 'great'.

Although we do call musicians who create music in other styles composers, the phrase 'The Great Composers' is usually used to refer to people who made music in any of the many European classical music styles from ca. 16th century to the 20th century.

Wolfgang Amadeus Mozart

Ludwig van Beethoven

Joseph Haydn

Johann Sebastian Bach

Richard Wagner

Need I go on?

It's a difficult club to break into, especially if you happen to be a person of colour or identify as any other gender apart from a cisgender man. When I say difficult, I mean almost impossible. That's one of the big issues with this idea of 'The Great Composers'. All of them are white, and they are from a small range of countries, including Germany, Austria, France, Italy, England, Russia, and the USA, from a certain period in ourstory.

Focusing on these white men and elevating them to demi-god status further perpetuates the idea that it is only these few white men who can ever lay claim to having made the best European classical music (which is, of course, the highest form of all music). Because this list of 'The Great Composers' doesn't change much at all, it also sends out another message — that people who do not identify as men, or people of colour, will never, and have never been able to create music on the same level as these white men.

In the world of sports, the idea of 'the greatest' changes with time (but not without much debate) in large part because there are clear metrics by which to measure teams or athletes. When Serena Williams retired in 2022, her number of Grand Slams and overall career wins meant that she joined the tennis GOAT conversation (Greatest Of All Time). When Tom Brady won his 7th Super Bowl title in 2021, this, alongside his many other records, set him apart from everyone else in American Football.

Usain Bolt's demolition of the 100m and 200m sprint records in 2009 solidified his place as the GOAT (for some). In music, we have no metrics to determine who deserves to be called the Greatest. If we can't say someone did something faster, higher, heavier, or accumulated more points, how do we measure greatness in music?

Number of instruments scored for?

Longest pieces?

Most streams?

Fastest solo?

Most amount of symphonies?

European imperialist attitudes dictated a desire to elevate those who fit certain ideals and philosophies of the day's dominant group. These people could be held up as those who were able to represent particular desirable ideals through musical composition. Popularity, political affiliation, and propaganda are all reasons one person may be regarded as great, and someone else not. In part, it's not just about how your music sounds, it's about who in positions of power likes it or sees a clear use for it.

It's this attitude that has helped to exclude people of colour and everyone else except for white men. Even though the British composer Samuel Coleridge-Taylor (of mixed Black and white heritage) was one of the most popular classical composers of the early 20th century, his contemporaries such as Gustav Holst or Ralph Vaughn Williams have a seat (or at least some of their compositions do) at the GOAT table. Although many women composers such as Rachel Portman, Clara Schumann, or Hannah Kendall have written incredibly moving or historically important music, that GOAT status remains out of reach.

It's important to remember that all of this is within the realm of European classical music. For people such as Miles Davis, Alice Coltrane, and J Dilla, that GOAT composer table has no seat for them — in fact, they reside in an entirely different building! If composers are composers, then there is no reason why some of the musicians who have taken a style of music and inspired, popularised, or innovated cannot also be called great. By only using the term 'Great Composers' when referring to composers of European classical music, it marks a clear separation between how we talk about composers in jazz or pop, and those centuries-old white men whose music is overrepresented in concerts around the world today. There is even a conversation to be had about how useful the phrase 'great' actually is.

There is no reason why Julius Eastman could not be sitting next to Mozart, as he asks Hildegard von Bingen to pass the butter, while Duke Ellington, Chen Yi, and Fela Kuti squabble over the last piece of pie.

Reflections

_____

_____

_____

_____

_____

_____

_____

_____

_____

_____

_____

_____

_____

_____

_____

_____

_____

Chapter 7

'Slaves'

If I were a racist,

I'd make sure that Gospel, Blues and Jazz,

Were always taught,

As music created by slaves.

So, if I mention the Trans-Atlantic Slave Trade in a lesson about the blues or jazz that makes me racist?

Not necessarily.

First of all, the idea of the word 'slave' has been contested in recent years. The word 'slave' or 'slaves' puts forward the idea that a person identifies as a slave and that slavery is their only way of life. The term 'enslaved' recognises a continual process that not only forced people into servitude but kept them in a state of subordination using different methods of punishment and laws for, in the context of the Trans-Atlantic Slave Trade, over 300 years. In addition to this, some of the laws and systems that were established back then are still affecting the descendants of enslaved peoples around the world to this day.

Gospel, blues, and jazz are styles of music that evolved at different times during the 19th and 20th centuries in the United States of America. They are primarily Black American artforms with roots in the rhythms, philosophies, and spirits of various forms from West Africa, with contributions from various other groups who migrated to the United States in the late 19th, and early 20th century. Of course, these ways of musicking arrived in America due to the Trans-Atlantic Slave Trade and subsequent industrialisation.

However, always referring to these forms as the music created by enslaved peoples erases the experiences of free Black people, either born or emancipated. It can also lead us to forget that gospel, blues, and jazz are still being made today, by fusing different styles and innovating older forms by people from all over the world.

It helps to feed the white supremacist narrative that there were benefits to slavery — if it wasn't for slavery, we wouldn't have gospel, blues, and jazz today. It also fails to recognise the struggles and experiences that created this music. The story of the blues is ultimately one of triumph in the face of oppression. Amongst other things, it is an example of how music can aid the struggle for freedom, while simultaneously providing a space for joy, expression, and catharsis.

If it wasn't for the resistance, imagination, and resilience of Black Americans in spite of being enslaved, we wouldn't have gospel, the blues, and jazz today.

See how different this is?

By avoiding the idea of 'enslaved' as opposed to 'slaves', we also avoid having to talk about power and race. Who enslaved who?

When, and for how long? Why did this happen? As the musician and educator Syreeta Neal once said, 'You can't teach the blues without talking about race and social justice'.

As previously discussed, whiteness embedded within music education has made it easy to avoid asking questions and thinking about subjects like this. Sometimes the way we think about a person, style of music, or a song can shift based on the reframing of a single word. While some may feel as though these subjects have no place in music education, it is up to those who believe in the importance of language to interrogate and equip themselves to handle certain conversations when they come up. It is important to create an environment where these conversations can happen organically, helping children and young people to understand the world and themselves a little bit better through the power of music.

Reflections

Chapter 8

World Music

If I were a racist,
I'd call all non-white music 'World Music'
After all,
It's them and us.

The term 'world music', was coined by the ethnomusicologist Robert E. Brown in the 1960s. In the 1980s, the phrase entered mainstream public consciousness (at least in the English-speaking world) and was used in the marketing of certain styles of music, both instrumental and vocal. If you went into a record shop before streaming services came about, the 'world music' aisle would contain CDs filled with music from various places around the world.

While this makes logical sense, there's a catch — *shouldn't all music be world music?*

'World music' usually refers to traditional and contemporary music that does not follow the chord patterns, rhythms, tuning, instrumentation, and spoken or sung English language of popular music from the Global North. It doesn't just mean the music of non-white peoples, as the music from countries such as Bulgaria, Spain, or Greece often falls into the 'World Music' category.

Depending on the culture you grew up in or in close proximity to, you may be used to Inuit throat singing, bhangra, or klezmer for example. You probably thought of these styles as... well, just music — not as a style within a category that could technically mean *anything*. The phrase 'world music' creates a paradigm which overwhelmingly positions the music of Black, Brown and Indigenous peoples from around the world as *other*. It's a phrase that divides our musical world along racial and socio-economic lines.

One of the interesting observations of 'world music' in education is how the silent influence of empire remains. For example, in UK music education, non-European classical music often focuses on styles from former colonies of the British empire — Jamaica (reggae), India (Carnatic/Hindustani/bhangra), and West Africa (drumming)[3]. Coincidence?

There is no equality in how many music education programmes focus on 'non-world music' and give very little time to 'world music'. As music curricula have been meticulously arranged and expanded over decades, it is not a coincidence that the music of white Europeans has been the main focus and also the lens through which much 'world music' is to be understood, analysed, and performed. When these musical styles sit within white spaces in this way, their meanings, contexts, and stories are often contorted in order to preserve these carefully constructed racial and epistemological hierarchies.

---

3   Although featured in UK music education, Indonesia (gamelan) was not a British Colony. However, the British controlled the island of Java from 1811-1816.

Despite many people wanting this to change, the challenge as to which styles are then to be focused on remains. With no consensus, limited resources, and training, only a surface-level understanding of many styles of music will continue to exist, unless there were to be significant investment — *but from who?*

Music education would look and sound very different, if a selection of styles from around the world were taught in equal measure, and not only through a Western classical lens and utilising staff notation. This approach could lead to a greater understanding of how different styles around the world have evolved, influenced each other, and need not be segregated and confined into racist categories such as 'world music'.

Reflections

_____

_____

_____

_____

_____

_____

_____

_____

_____

_____

_____

_____

_____

_____

_____

_____

_____

_____

Chapter 9

Classical Music & The Trans-Atlantic Slave Trade

If I were a racist,
I'd ignore that Mozart, Beethoven, Haydn, Bach,
And the Trans-Atlantic Slave Trade
Happened at the same time.

Context can change everything. When we begin to understand how aspects of our lives, societies, music, and ourstory are connected, we can experience pieces of music or view composers from a different angle. These various perspectives help us to piece together the complex puzzle that is humanity, as opposed to focusing on the supposed absolutism of music.

During the 17th and 18th centuries, European colonial powers exploited the natural resources, and peoples from places around the world and amassed great wealth and power. Precious metals, spices, and other resources were shipped back to England, France, Spain, and other countries and territories, which when sold, lined the pockets of many. This influx in wealth directly funded European industrialisation and gave some of the wealthiest people extra money to spend on the arts.

For many different reasons, including the widespread use

of print media and the wider availability and evolution of instruments, there was a musical boom. More money resulted in the ability for composers and musicians to earn a living from their artistry, compositions, and performances. The widespread nature of the colonial enterprise meant that churches and other Christian institutions profited and were subsequently able to employ more and more musicians.

Often, white supremacy will allow us to see and even discuss the surface effects of racism or colonialism but obscure the ways in which racism and the effects of colonialism have infiltrated many aspects of our lives — musical or otherwise. In many cases, the flow of money has been covered up or lost, and in recent times, companies and even whole countries have issued apologies, acknowledging how they have benefitted financially from the Trans-Atlantic Slave Trade. All of this is not to say that every Western European composer of the time was directly connected to slavery — but by virtue of living in certain countries and territories, and the business of their patrons, there is no doubt that many benefitted indirectly off the backs of enslaved peoples.

In some ways, George Frideric Handel personifies the complex nature of these connections. In 2013, Librarian Emeritus David Hunter found the composers signature against three buy/sell orders for stock in the Royal African Company[4] in 1720[5]. In addition to this, Hunter suggests that without the support of

---

4   The Royal African Company was charted in 1672 by King Charles II and his brother, the future King James II. Its main purpose was to trade for enslaved peoples, gold, ivory and other resources.
5   Robin, W. (Host). (2021, May). Handel and the Slave Trade with David Hunter. *Sound Expertise.* https://open.spotify.com/episode/1GWZEmLHKTwfRmM8oG9lnR?si=9947569cb0614261

the 1st Duke of Chandos, James Brydges (who himself had a controlling stake in the RAC), Handel may not have had the opportunity to craft the musical works and forms which are beloved the world over. Further investigation reveals links between investors in the RAC and investors in the Royal Academy of Music, one of the worlds most renowned music teaching institutions.

It is sobering to realise that while some celebrate the achievements and music of many composers at this time in ourstory, at the very same time, others are forced to remember their ancestors being enslaved, beaten, tortured, and murdered. It's a reminder that there are always multiple stories happening at the same time.

On the 21st of August 1791, the Haitian Revolution began, marking the start of the most successful slave rebellion connected to the Trans-Atlantic Slave Trade. Just over a month later on the 30th of September 1791, Mozart's opera *The Magic Flute* premiered. While this doesn't mean that every time we talk, analyse, or listen to the music of Mozart et al., we need to mention these facts, we should, at the very least, be aware of these larger contexts.

In school, I wondered why it seemed as though there were no people of colour making music at this time. Of course, there were, but since we never came across any of them, I (and many others) assumed that there just weren't any. I later went on to learn about Chevalier de Saint George, Ignatius Sancho, George Bridgewater, and others who made music in various European classical styles. Their absence from 'mainstream' musical history alongside the epistemological and physical violence enacted on people of colour at this time, means that music from the Global South has never been recognised as coming anywhere close to the *works* created by these 'Great Composers'.

It's not just about the Trans-Atlantic Slave Trade and anti-blackness. The late 19th century saw a rise of anti-semitism and nationalism in Europe, which was during the time of Richard Wagner, Claude Debussy, Johann Strauss, and Pyotr Ilyich Tchaikovsky. Apartheid in South Africa lasted from 1948 — 1994, during a time in which styles such as rock, pop, and jazz flourished around the world. We can choose to study various styles of music without their wider socio-political contexts, but when we bring them in, they reveal brand-new meanings and perspectives. Doing so represents a step towards acknowledging the oppression and triumph that have created the world we live in today.

Reflections

Chapter 10

Instruments

If I were a racist,
I'd make sure that violins and pianos
Were seen as more important,
Than Steel pans, tablas, and didgeridoos.

If a child said that they wanted to play an instrument and had two options available — the piano or tabla — which one might you recommend? How about a steel pan or guitar? Cello or sitar? Bass guitar or guzheng?

Due to the availability and affordability of many different instruments, it's often the pianos, violins, and cellos (instruments of the European orchestra) that get picked first. Following those come instruments most commonly heard in popular music styles, such as guitars, basses, and drum kits. It makes a degree of sense. In the Global North, much of our musical lives are dominated by certain instruments, the sounds they make, and one system of tuning. In many churches and schools, the main instruments used are usually pianos, organs, or guitars. The first songs played and created for early years and primary age children usually involve pianos and guitars, before moving on to listen to various other styles of music from around the world that often use similar instruments. The styles of music given the most prestige in our societies are often various forms of European classical music, and these are the instruments that are given priority. Our musical world is set up for us to seek out the cultural capital that comes with instruments of the European orchestra.

If we were to treat shakuhachis, sarods, or didgeridoos in the same way, it would totally transform the way we teach and learn about music, especially in the Global North. We'd begin to become more familiar with various ways of tuning, language, philosophies, and movement, and how these instruments and music are embedded and embodied in various cultures. Having the option to gain internationally recognised qualifications by playing these instruments would allow for a greater variety of people to access and feel welcome in institutionalised music education. It would also create a bigger demand for instruments from the Global South, providing more people around the world with the opportunity to earn a living from making, repairing, and teaching how to play these instruments.

Maintaining the focus on violins, pianos, and other orchestral instruments, centres whiteness and those in positions of power who profit from the creation of these musical instruments. It encourages the attitude that steel pans, tablas, and djembes can remain 'interesting world music instruments' but must always come secondary when it's time for the serious business of learning and teaching about music.

Reflections

Chapter 11

'African' Songs

If I were a racist,
I'd teach 'African' songs,
Without knowing what they mean,
Or where they were really from.

In Chapter 4, I explored the idea of 'African drumming', and how by using terms like this, we make many assumptions, and effectively homogenise the musical output of an entire continent.

The issue with 'African' songs is similar. There are songs that can be found in much of the repertoire in music education that have simply been labelled as 'African'. Not West African, East African, Central, or Southern — just 'African'. Imagine a song that was described as being traditional European. Or traditional Asian. How about traditional South American? It's lazy at best, racist at worst. Not only because we are talking about a large geographical region but also because these tunes are often labelled without a timeframe attached. In theory, a 'traditional African' song could mean from Madagascar, composed in 1392, or from Algeria in 1906. If we wouldn't accept (or even come across) a song labelled 'European', then why should we accept the same for Africa?

But what to do with all the music currently labelled like this? One of the issues with certain songs is that some were transcribed by people who visited various places in Africa and brought them back to Europe, Canada, the U.S., and other places to teach. Over time, some of these songs have been repeated and taught, while their original contexts and meanings have faded from memory.

While possibly unintentional, many songs from Africa, Asia, the Caribbean, South America, and the Indigenous peoples of North America and Oceania have been printed, sold, taught, and performed without critical scrutiny. The manifestation of whiteness within the music education ecosystem means that it was rarely seen as a problem to label a song as 'African'. These labels also serve another purpose — they tacitly reinforce the idea that songs like these are found around Africa and sung regularly. It also hints at the idea that there were/are no singular composers, and documenting when or where a song was created is something that Africans are unable to do through a lack of understanding or technology — in short, an 'uncivilised' approach to music making.

Another factor to consider is the relatively recent establishment of many African countries. Nations like Ghana were once composed of distinct tribes, each governing its own territories, until European colonists arrived and delineated the borders we recognise today. Consequently, numerous 'traditional' Ghanaian songs may actually trace their origins to present-day Togo, Côte d'Ivoire, or Burkina Faso.

Songs are labelled like this in part because many educators and publishers feel safe in the knowledge that by teaching these songs, children are learning about the building blocks of music — texture, timbre, tempo, and rhythm. Sometimes this means teaching songs without knowing their meaning as they are in a different language, with no translations and few online resources. Unlike songs with racist histories, while the translations may not contain harmful lyrics, it is the act of teaching something without a basic understanding of its context that upholds the lower required standards that whiteness sets for groups other than its own.

Ideally, the information about when these songs were written, who wrote them, the languages they are in, and translations would be easily available. The decisions about gathering this kind of information often come down to economics — which organisations will pay for the research, contextualisation, and design of these resources, and who will subsequently profit from them?

As Martin Urbach writes,

At the core, what needs to be addressed is the system of white supremacy which allowed for minstrel songs and other racist songs to make it into the songbooks the teacher training programs we teachers pay thousands of dollars to learn from to be normalized and accepted as 'the norm'.[6]

Until we are honest about how the economics of music education impact what is taught, songs labelled 'African' may be taken out, but they will be replaced by silence.

---

6   Martin Urbach's 2019 essay entitled '"You Might Be Left With Silence When You're Done"; The White Fear of Taking Racist Songs Out of Music Education' expands on this point - https://medium.com/@martinurbach/you-might-be-left-with-silence-when-youre-done-the-white-fear-of-taking-racist-songs-out-of-89ecdc300ee5 (Accessed: 8 Oct 2023)

Reflections

_____

_____

_____

_____

_____

_____

_____

_____

_____

_____

_____

_____

_____

_____

_____

_____

_____

_____

_____

_____

Chapter 12

Tuning

If I were a racist,
I'd standardise everything –
You're either in tune,
Or you're out. Literally.

There are so many things we take for granted in music education. One of the fundamental things is how we tune our instruments — it's a system that's not as universal or even as old as we might think.

The note 'A' tuned at 440Hz was formalised by the International Organisation for Standardisation in 1975[7], but instruments that conformed to this way of tuning were being made before then. It's extremely useful to have a standard tuning system — it means that people from around the world can play together within it. It also allows for musical ideas to be shared and understood in similar ways around the world. Equal temperament, which was developed in 16th century China, divided the octave into 12 equal parts. This system is the one that many people around the world

---

7   Zimmerman, A. (2020). A Chronicle of Sound-Establishing Community. https://theslg.com/img/cms/ frequenciespdf/A%20Chronicle%20of%20Sound-Establishing%20Community.pdf. (Accessed: 29 Nov 2023)

are most familiar with, although other systems are used, often in the Global South.

As many people around the world are now used to the twelve notes in a scale and A=440Hz, this has become the sonic foundation upon which much (if not all) of music education is based. This is not to say that it is inherently bad — it is to say that is way of musicking excludes ways in which many people create and experience music. It goes without saying that this disproportionately affects the music created by people in the Global South.

The issues of tuning and equal temperament are complicated ones and change in this area can be extremely tough. Recognising the problem, people such as Khyam Allami have created software that allows its users to compose using various tuning and temperament systems[8]. These technologies are extremely important. Not only does it help the people whose music usually sits outside of music education to finally have the technology to create certain styles of music, but it also offers those who may not be familiar with certain styles of music the opportunity to dive into other sound worlds in a more authentic way.

---

[8]   Khyam Allami's free to access online software called Leimma and Apothem can be found at https://isartum.net/

Reflections

Chapter 13

Representation

If I were a racist,
I'd have posters of me on the walls and in the books.
No black or brown faces,
Just my own.

If I wanted you to believe that the best music worth studying, analysing, and learning was the music that I value the most, I'd make sure that it wasn't just about what you heard. I'd make sure that everywhere you looked, you'd see white people, and particularly white cisgender men in books, resources, and posters who teach about various forms and elements of music. I'd want you to see these faces all the time — so much so that if you ever saw someone who wasn't a white man, you'd either be very excited or think that white men were being marginalised or erased.

In seeking to further understand how to influence consumers, one of the ideas suggested by Herbert E. Krugman was the 'mere exposure effect'[9], which was developed by people such as Gustav Fechner and Robert Zajonc in the late 19th and early 20th centuries. The idea is that repeated exposure to a subject

---

9   Krugman, H. E. (1968). Processes underlying exposure to advertising. *American Psychologist, 23*(4), 245–253. https://doi.org/10.1037/h0026247

or idea can increase your tendency to like it, even when minimal attention is paid to it. It is a form of conditioning, as we take in information all the time, becoming gradually unaware that the faces or images we are exposed to, are slowly layering and entrenching our biases on an unconscious level.

Representation is important for many reasons. It is important that people are able to see and identify in various ways with musicians, producers, and teachers past and present. For some people, that can be the difference between pursuing a style of music or playing a particular instrument. For others, it could simply help to put a crack in stereotypes and assumptions, realising that many different kinds of people have made incredible music.

However, representation by itself may not be enough. Under white supremacy, we can often believe that simply adding a Yoko Kanno, Clarice Assad, or A.R. Rahman to repertoire or posters fixes the problem. Adding a variety of composers doesn't necessarily change the approaches, frameworks, and basic assumptions that many of us have when we talk about certain styles of music. The faces may look 'different', but the analysis, performance aesthetics and pedagogies remains the same.

Without taking the time to understand the struggles, triumphs, ourstories, subject matter, and relationships that created cultures and societies, representation may only remain surface level and therefore, tokenistic.

There are also other questions about which aspects of someone's identity might be representative. For example, just because we may see a woman of South Asian heritage, it doesn't mean that all girls of the same heritage will automatically feel represented or connected to them. As Christopher Emdin writes, there are many people who feel more connected to their local environments and cultures, than the cultures connected to their various countries of heritage.[10]

By constantly seeing white cisgender men on walls and in books, we can falsely begin to make assumptions about who can do something and who is important enough to be looked at, studied, and listened to on a regular basis. Combating these ideas not only means changing who we see, listen to, and analyse in classrooms, but also the underlying ideas, approaches and knowledges that have shaped our musical world.

---

10   Emdin C. (2016). For white folks who teach in the hood— and the rest of y'all too : reality pedagogy and urban education. Beacon Press.

Reflections

Chapter 14

DEI

If I were a racist,
I'd make you think including one brown face,
Would be enough.
Diversity. Inclusion.

In recent years, DEI, EDI, IDEA, and other acronyms have increased in use, with many organisations attempting to try and diversify, include, and increase representation. Many have taken concrete steps by hiring historically marginalised peoples, or creating resources, such as books or posters which feature more people who belong to groups who have been historically marginalised and oppressed. In some ways, it has been a positive shift, with increased awareness about race and white supremacy, improved complaints procedures, more music by Black, Brown and Indigenous composers, and an increasing sense of being heard and seen. In some ways, however, it has further entrenched racist ideologies and further polarised the political left and right.

Unfortunately, this has not all come about because of careful research, new evidence, or a general awakening, but out of fear and worry. As the murder of George Floyd coincided with the global COVID-19 pandemic, many people were forced to confront issues of race for the first time. Many DEI working groups and committees were set up in order to analyse their governance, diversify, be more inclusive, and work towards equitable opportunities and outcomes. While some faces may have changed, some of the attitudes and approaches have not.

Whiteness is not only the preserve of white people. The same racist ideas and oppressive practices can be enacted by Black, Brown and Indigenous peoples, often under the guise of promoting a colour-blind society. Wealth and power can create blinders that can cause people to perpetuate the very same policies and ideologies that have marginalised and oppressed their own people.

While many of these endeavours helped in different ways (even if they only allowed companies to make public statements about their work), real change isn't about seeing one or two brown, non cis-het faces. It is about challenging the basic assumptions and knowledges that are perpetuated by dominant cultures on local, national, and international levels. It's about understanding how the past informs and shapes the present. Just because there may be an increase of oppressed minorities in any setting, it doesn't necessarily mean that everything is or will be better.

These are just a few examples of conversations and questions that are important to have in today's society and in music education. It all begins with individuals understanding that the world in its present state is the product of many choices, oppression, and opportunism, and not the result of any form of natural selection. If oppression and marginalisation have created oppressive systems over time, these same systems will need to evolve or be destroyed and rebuilt in order to prevent further damage — systems that are built upon the knowledge and experiences of all stakeholders.

It is here that ideas associated with decolonisation offers additional ideas and perspectives that go beyond race. Decolonisation - the process of uncovering, analysing and moving away from colonial structures (material and epistemological) as created during the European colonial era, gives us a lens in which to create a plurality of ways of teaching and learning about music. It then no longer becomes about adding people to a system not designed for them, but allows for people to bring their knowledges and ways of being into intuitions and classrooms.

It is important to consider how DEI approaches can help transform and reinvigorate music education. It's also important to be critical of these same approaches, and search for deeper answers to our questions.

Reflections

Chapter 15

The Best

If I were a racist,
I'd be fine with all white exam boards,
And all white teaching staff,
And study all white musicians.

One of the ways in which white supremacy manifests is
through the idea that the output of certain people represents
the best that humanity has to offer. This has usually meant that
the literature, music, art, philosophies, and technology created or
appropriated by white cis-hetero European men have been held up
as the universal standard. However, to explicitly say this would
be openly racist and misogynist. Instead, what we see are these
ideas quietly embedded within music education, protected under
the guise of being 'the best'.

We learn through those musicians who have used instruments
in innovative ways, crafted grand melodies, interesting harmonies,
or sold millions of records. Since they are the people who are
required to be studied, they tacitly become the most important,
and logically, if children are to learn, they should only learn from
the best. If anything else were to be added to this established best,
one then runs the risk of diminishing the perceived overall quality

of the syllabus, curriculum, or repertoire. Using Beethoven as an example, Philip Ewell writes:

> *Beethoven was undoubtedly an above-average composer and he deserves our attention. But to say he was anything more is to dismiss 99.9% of the world's music written 200+ years ago, which would be unscholarly, and academically irresponsible.*[11]

When we examine the stories of composers such as J.S. Bach or Mozart, we start to see how these men were not geniuses who would have flourished regardless of their gender, sexuality, place, and time they were born, but men who were able to take advantage of the privileges afforded to them. If Mozart was born in 1756 but in the region now known as Iran, it is doubtful that he would be regarded as a brilliant composer in spite of the style of music he may have created. His status as being one of the best, cannot be separated from the environment he was born into.

While many may not claim that having syllabi or curricula that only feature white people is racist, the question then has to be asked — Why does the output of non-white peoples remain marginalised or excluded? As mentioned in Chapter 5, without clearly being able to measure 'the best', questions must be asked why 'the best' tends to have been created by this particular homogenous group of people. Similar issues can also be found in recruitment. What happens when the 'best' candidates, and subsequently those who go on to become heads

---

11   Ewell, P. (2020). 'Beethoven was an above-average composer, let's leave it at that', Music Theory's White Racial Frame, 24 April, Available at: https://musictheoryswhiteracialframe.wordpress.com/2020/04/24/beethoven-was-an-above-average-composer-lets-leave-it-at-that/ (Accessed: 13 June 2023)

of departments, senior lecturers, professors, and CEOs in the music industry are an overwhelmingly homogenous group?

Studying only white musicians can be a diverse experience, as race is not the beginning and the end of identity. However, learning about the music created by Black, Brown and Indigenous, disabled, LGBTQIA2S+, and other marginalised peoples will only make the teaching and learning experience richer and wider. What are the stories, techniques, sounds, and feelings we miss out on if we only concentrate on those who are currently regarded as 'the best'? Should the idea of the best or greatest even exist?

Reflections

Chapter 16

Western Music Notation

If I were a racist,
I would insist that children learn Western music notation,
Forgetting that many civilisations,
Flourished without it for centuries.

Music notation is a brilliant thing. For those who can decipher the specific lines, words, and dots, it's a system that allows people from all over the world to play a particular piece of music. Groups of people can get together and play the same piece of music straightaway, each with different parts which, when played accurately, can create a wonderful tapestry of sound.

But the question is, which music notation am I referring to?

There are many different ways that instructions on how to play a particular piece or express an idea have been created throughout human existence. The musician and researcher Jon Silpayamanant has complied a blog which lists over 900 different notation systems from around the world to date[12]. When we say music notation, in theory (no pun intended), we could be talking about any of these 900+ systems but often we aren't. Often, we

---

12   Silpayamanant, J. (2017). 'Timeline of Music Notation', Silpayamanant's Weblog, Available at: https://silpayamanant.wordpress.com/timeline-of-music-notation/ Accessed: 10 Sept 2023.

only focus on the Western European system, which I'll refer to as staff notation.

While this system is extremely useful, it has its limitations. There's a video by the YouTuber 12tone called 'How Sheet Music Lies to You'[13], which goes into detail about staff notation, and how there are so many things that it can't tell us about a piece of music and how to interpret it, without the page potentially becoming illegible. When we only ever teach from notation, key elements of music such as groove, velocity, harmonics, ghost notes, the specific amount of vibrato, or the colour of a note (relative to another) can be very difficult to convey.

Staff notation was created in large part to aid the production and performance of Western European classical music. Even for other styles developed in the Global North such as the blues, hip hop, or even pop, it isn't optimal, let alone for any other styles found around the world. The pulling and pushing of rhythms and time, halftones, colours, and other nuances of performance just can't be represented clearly and efficiently using staff notation.

This way of musicking upholds white supremacy by insisting that all music is taught through and learned by understanding

the particular symbols of staff notation. Many music education programs and curricula around the world are based on the premise that children and young people need to learn how to

13   Arnold, C. [12tone] (2022) 'How Sheet Music Lies To You', Available at: https://www.youtube.com/watch?v=quOLtEOwfAo&t=472s. (Accessed: 20 Oct 2023)

read this type of notation. It also means that it can be difficult to become a music teacher if you find it difficult to understand.

This system, which evolved in Europe over hundreds of years, is now the main system used around the world to enter certain music examinations and gain access to many degree programs. It is built into the music industry ecosystem, with millions of dollars being spent each year on the printing and online distribution of sheet music written using staff notation. Other ways of notating music or learning by ear are treated as secondary. This is a not-so-subtle form of institutionalised racism — the building of economic structures and education which, on many levels, disproportionally affects Black, Brown and Indigenous peoples around the world. It creates cycles which (as previously discussed) affect who can become a music teacher, and therefore, who is present when syllabi and curricula are being reviewed, created, and produced. This increases the potential for certain nuances to be lost, and racist songs/phrases going unnoticed, albeit passing through the hands of well-meaning white people.

It can be extremely advantageous to be able to read staff notation but not being able to can result in many people feeling as though they can't be musicians, and therefore, they don't go on to study music. Of course, many musicians throughout ourstory have had incredible careers without being able to read any kind of notation, but in mainstream education, the barriers still remain. It does not simplify or reduce the quality of music education to give more time to explore and understand various ways to notate music. In fact, it would enhance the teaching and learning experience if there were more flexibility in how teachers and students represented the sounds that they want to hear, or have heard on paper, or on any other medium.

The rise of music education on YouTube and other streaming platforms that can teach users how to play a piece or improvise without using staff notation raises questions around why someone needs to go to college or university to learn the intricacies of a certain style of music. Why invest the time and money to learn to read staff notation, when I can learn how to play the music I want, at the pace I want, where I want, and for very little cost?

Music will always thrive, as it always has done for centuries without staff notation. The question is whether music education in schools, colleges, and universities will begin to recognise the legitimacy of other ways of expressing and documenting music. What are the potential ramifications if they don't?

Reflections

Chapter 17

Training

If I were a racist,
I'd put up black squares,
And messages about standing together.
Then never invest in anti-racism training for my staff.

The 2nd June 2020, marked #BlackoutTuesday. On that day, many people and organisations posted black squares on social media platforms to show support for the Black Lives Matter movement, less than two weeks after the murder of George Floyd. While this showed a level of engagement and understanding, it was to be what happened afterwards that was most significant.

In the aftermath, many people felt as though the situation for Black people hadn't really changed much. In some sense, the black squares did what they were supposed to — it showed support. For many, the support lacked genuine commitment to confront and to change.

Investing in anti-racism training can also just be another way to show support without actually doing anything. Hiring someone to talk about our story of racism and its real-life effects can sometimes work out more in favour of those who don't experience racism than those who do. Many Black people were put on the spot, and overnight, assumed unpaid 'diversity' roles or felt additional pressure to have to speak about certain triggering situations and issues in public. Having conversations and educating ourselves about these topics is important, but it is what we do with the information that is crucial.

Anti-racism is a stance — it means continually being aware of how racism has embedded itself in many ways into our society and actively trying to uncover, stop, and reverse it. In terms of music education, it's to understand how racism manifests in resources, pedagogy, recruitment, training, and testing, and seeking ways to uncover and curtail its effects. If we take anti-racism in all its forms seriously, investment into new resources, structures, hiring practices, and other facets of music education need to be a priority. We must also remember that our institutions are a reflection of the society that they are formed from. An anti-racist music education cannot exist without thorough investigation and awareness of how racism has, can, does and will continue to play a part in the society it is based in.

Anti-racism is incredibly complex and layered - it requires constant growth and continuous development. The symptoms and structures of 400+ years of pseudo-scientific racism, propaganda, and stereotyping will not go away after a social media post, a diversity statement, and a 2-hour workshop.

Reflections

Chapter 18

Allyship

If I were a racist,
I wouldn't address outdated policies
Or really let black and brown people
feel safe enough to speak on their experiences.

Going beyond anti-racist gestures and statements is key to helping people to feel safe enough to give voice to their experiences. It is one thing to put up black squares (such as more Black or Brown faces on websites or flyers), but it is yet another to really attempt to understand how the experiences of employees, students, or co-workers may be impacted by everyday interactions and policies. It's not as simple as declaring that office doors are open or designating a Black or Brown person to be an unpaid diversity officer.

Being an ally means consistently taking a proactive stance against racism. It means that when we see music education resources that contain racist or questionable content, we flag it up in our music education communities. If there are questions that need asking, it means that we need to be careful about how to understand the experience of historically oppressed peoples better. By naming specific problems and ideas rather than avoiding the use of words or phrases (white supremacy, for example), we can begin to see how important language can be in fighting against racism.

There are so many books, podcasts, articles, and videos that contain valuable information about racism and how to be an ally. Allyship requires us to learn from various sources without being asked to, and not depending on oppressed peoples to be a free source of information. By learning how to decentre ourselves, we can begin to give new meanings to the information we come across. We can learn to understand that what may simply be mildly interesting or trivial to one person, may hold significant importance for another. It is an uncomfortable but necessary process to understand internalised whiteness, homophobia, or misogynoir for example. In doing so, we can deepen our understanding of the subtle and overt ways that white supremacy manifests itself in music education. It must be said, white saviourism is real and should be considered, especially whenever majority-white institutions and companies try to diversify, include, or decolonise.

Because racism is not just about name calling, having an understanding of the different elements of who we are and the privilege and power that comes with it is important. Critiquing our own positionalities can help us to understand how racism manifests systemically and bestows privileges cloaked in ideas of meritocracy. It means understanding that we all have a part to play in dismantling and confronting this thing called racism.

Reflections

Chapter 19

White Spaces

If I were a racist,
I'd know that,
Even though the notes may be black,
The spaces would remain white.

The reality is that in the Global North, the majority of students will be taught by white people, and the majority of people making the most important decisions in society will be white. White spaces are one thing. Spaces that perpetuate whiteness are something different.

It is the latter that has created a system that harms people of colour disproportionally, and employs a deficit model in which those oppressed peoples are solely responsible for the situations they find themselves in. It means that even with all the will in the world, it is impossible for one or two white people in an all-white organisation to create the changes needed for Black, Brown and Indigenous people to thrive in many different ways.

Black, Brown and Indigenous peoples have always worked, and even flourished in white spaces, often having to adjust, code switch, and hide parts of their identities and experiences in order to fit in. The hope is that by doing the work to understand, white people realise the power they have to transform, break, and dismantle these structures. This should not be carried out by white people alone, as Paulo Freire in *Pedagogy of the Oppressed*[14] makes clear. By doing so in partnership with oppressed peoples, racism embedded in systems and pedagogy can begin to be properly addressed.

A music education that allows students to talk about music in the ways that are familiar to them.

A music education that is not afraid to touch on politics, even the songs or people who speak directly to white supremacy.

A music education that is as specific as possible when talking about music from the Global South.

A music education that recognises and studies the music of a variety of peoples, regardless of their race, gender, or sexual orientation.

A music education that understands quality — not as a universal standard, but is time, style, and context-specific.

A music education that embraces the humanity of all, acknowledging struggles and triumphs, and doesn't view people as the result of some of the darkest moments in the story of humankind.

A music education that understands all music has emerged from the world and deserves to be treated equally and studied through its own lens.

---

14   Freire, P. (1970) *Pedagogy of the Oppressed*, Continuum.

A music education that respects a variety of instruments and doesn't penalise those who don't play orchestral instruments.

A music education that seeks to be culturally relevant.

A music education that embraces many forms of notation and allows those who learn by ear to use those skills without having to learn staff notation to progress.

A music education that is structured to address past inequalities and uplift the most marginalised in our communities.

A music education that understands its purpose and shapes the pedagogy, hires, and trains the right people to carry that purpose out.

All of this and more is possible. With consistent efforts to understand the impacts of racism on our profession, we can create a better music education ecosystem for historically marginalised folks. Ultimately, doing this will benefit every single individual who arrives in a music classroom, eager to harness the power of music to express and connect with themselves, the people around them, and the world.

Reflections

References

African Union Mission to the United Nations (2020) *The Africa Group at the United Nations*. African Union. https://www.africanunion-un.org/africangroup#:~:text=The%20Africa%20Group%20at%20the,States%20at%20the%20United%20Nations. (Accessed 23 Oct 2023).

Arnold, C. [12tone] (2022). *'How Sheet Music Lies To You'*, Available at: https://www.youtube.com/watch?v=quOLtE0wfAo&t=472s. (Accessed: 20 Oct 2023).

Emdin C. (2016). For white folks who teach in the hood-- and the rest of y'all too : reality pedagogy and urban education. Beacon Press.

Ewell, P. (2020). 'Beethoven was an above-average composer, let's leave it at that', Music Theory's White Racial Frame, 24 April, Available at: https://musictheoryswhiteracialframe.wordpress.com/2020/04/24/beethoven-was-an-above-average-composer-lets-leave-it-at-that/ (Accessed: 13 June 2023)

Freire, P. (1970). *Pedagogy of the Oppressed*, Continuum.

Krugman, H. E. (1968). Processes underlying exposure to advertising. *American Psychologist*, 23(4), 245–253. https://doi.org/10.1037/h0026247

Market Growth Reports (2023). *Global Sheet Music Market Size, Star and Industry Analysis by regions, Countries, Types, and Applications, Forecast to 2028*. Market Growth Reports.

Mitchell, M. D. (2013). "Legitimate commerce" in the Eighteenth Century: The Royal African Company of England Under the Duke of Chandos, 1720–1726. *Enterprise & Society, 14*(3), 544–578. https://doi.org/10.1093/es/kht038

Robin, W. (Host). (2021, May). Handel and the Slave Trade with David Hunter. *Sound Expertise.* https://open.spotify.comepisode/1GWZEmLHKTwfRmM8oG9lnR?si=9947569cb0614261

Silpayamanant, J. (2017). 'Timeline of Music Notation', Silpayamanant's Weblog, Available at: https://silpayamanant.wordpress.com/timeline-of-music-notation/ (Accessed: 10 Sept 2023).

Urbach, M. (2019). *'You Might Be Left With Silence When You're Done'; The White Fear of Taking Racist Songs Out of Music Education..*, *Medium.* Available at: https://medium.com/@martinurbach/you-might-be-left-with-silence-when-youre-done-the-white-fear-of-taking-racist-songs-out-of-89ecdc300ee5 (Accessed: 8 Oct 2023).

Zimmerman, A. (2020). A Chronicle of Sound-Establishing Community. https://theslg.com/img/cms/frequenciespdf/A%20Chronicle%20of%20Sound-Establishing%20Community.pdf. (Accessed: 29 Nov 2023)

Milton Keynes UK
Ingram Content Group UK Ltd.
UKHW020620220424
441543UK00007B/116

9 781739 583958